DR. CLEMENT OGUNYEMI

NINE TENTH

Cover Design: Joshua Ogunyemi

Nine Tenth: Church Folks' Guide to Financial Discipline & Living Beyond Tithes & Offering

CONGRATULATIONS!!
You have taken the 1st steps in achieving your financial freedom and becoming a financially literate individual or family. It is my pleasure to be able to guide you through this process and provide you with the tools necessary to make it to the end of your journey. I hope that by the end of this session, you can take these principles and concepts and apply them to your daily life. More importantly, I hope that your financial health will be improved and that you move from the death grips of debt and poor financial decision-making, to a worry-free life of financial freedom.

Yours Truly,

Dr. Clement O. Ogunyemi
4Q Pro Financial Management & Consulting, LLC
www.4qfinancial.com

TABLE OF CONTENTS

Introduction

2 Corinthians 9:7 *- ...For God loves a cheerful giver.*

Genesis 28:22 *- ...And of all that you give me I will give a full tenth to you."*

From adolescence, we have been taught to give the 1st tenth of our earnings in the form of tithes. Furthermore, we've been taught to do so *CHEERFULLY*. For many of us going through the motions, we return home only to be faced with a not-so-cheerful reality that our finances **SUCK**. Whether we are living paycheck to paycheck or receive government assistance, the cheer of giving is often overshadowed by a grim financial situation. If we are only trained to give the 1st tenth, how are we struggling with nine tenths? Why has no one taught us what to do with the remainder of our money, the nine tenths? Very good questions! I'm here to walk you through being, not only good, but GREAT, stewards of the money that you have been blessed with. Welcome to the best advice you will ever receive.

Welcome to financial freedom!

Before we get started, let's set the scene with an all-to-familiar story.

Linda's Story

Let's look at an example:

Linda is a 32-year-old, single mother of two. It's Sunday. While riding the emotional high of the great word that was preached, and listening to uplifting songs ministered by the choir, Linda, with her regular tithes in hand, reaches *back* into her purse, digs out the envelope marked with big red letters "**GAS MONEY**", and dances her way down the aisle to the offering table. Most see this as an act of FAITH. However, soon after Sister Linda gives what is her last twenty dollars, she realizes that she *may* not be able to drive to work this week; she *may* not be able to pay her already late light or water bills.

Down from her emotional high and on the drive home, she begins to panic and becomes quite anxious. "What have I done?", she thought. "My kids and I will be sitting in a cold, dark house...with no water!" *Oh, Linda Linda Linda...*

Now, I am NOT by any means saying that giving tithes and offering is wrong.

We, Christians, believe that God's Word ordains it. On the other hand (in the same Bible), God teaches us to be good stewards. AND that if we can be good stewards of the little that we have, He will make us MASTERS over much more.

Moral of the story? Giving tithe and offering without FIRST devising a plan is a BAD idea.

Planning Questionnaire

Who is responsible for day-to-day financial decisions in your household?

a. You
b. You & Your Partner
c. You & Another Family Member
d. Your Partner
e. Another Family Member
f. Someone Else
g. Nobody

Does your household have a budget?

a. Yes
b. No
c. Not Sure

I carefully consider whether or not I can afford something before buying it.

a. Completely Agree
b. Somewhat Agree
c. Agree
d. Somewhat Disagree
e. Disagree
f. Completely Disagree

The next few pages will help you take the first steps toward financial freedom. —>

I tend to live for today and let tomorrow take care of itself.
a. Completely Agree
b. Somewhat Agree
c. Agree
d. Somewhat Disagree
e. Disagree
f. Completely Disagree

I find it more satisfying to spend money than to save it for the long-term.
a. Completely Agree
b. Somewhat Agree
c. Agree
d. Somewhat Disagree
e. Disagree
f. Completely Disagree

I pay my bills on time.
a. Completely Agree
b. Somewhat Agree
c. Agree
d. Somewhat Disagree
e. Disagree
f. Completely Disagree

I keep a close, personal watch on my finances.
a. Completely Agree
b. Somewhat Agree
c. Agree
d. Somewhat Disagree
e. Disagree
f. Completely Disagree

I set long-term financial goals and strive to achieve them.
a. Completely Agree
b. Somewhat Agree
c. Agree
d. Somewhat Disagree
e. Disagree
f. Completely Disagree

Money is there to be spent.
a. Completely Agree
b. Somewhat Agree
c. Agree
d. Somewhat Disagree
e. Disagree
f. Completely Disagree

Sometimes people find that their income doesn't quite cover their living costs.
In the last 12 months this has happened to me.

a. Yes
b. No
c. Not Sure

Tithes and offering are extremely important to me.

a. Yes
b. No

I give my tithes and offering even when I may not have enough to pay my bills.

a. Sometimes
b. Always
c. Never

My Top 5 Personal Goals Are:

1. _____

2. _____

3. _____

4. _____

5. _____

Now that you know where you stand, let's discuss "Building a Solid Financial House."

*"I will show you what it's like when someone comes to me, listens to my teaching, and then follows it. It's like a person building a house that digs deep and lays the foundation on **solid** rock. When the floodwaters rise and break against that house, it stands **firm** because it is well built. However, anyone who hears and doesn't obey is like a person who builds a house right on the ground, without a foundation. When the floods sweep down against that house, it will collapse into a heap of ruins."*

- Luke 6:47-49 (NLT)

Building a _Solid_ Financial House

J ust as any architect and THE Architect understand, a solid foundation is imperative to having an infrastructure that can withstand severe wind and weather. The same can be said when preparing to build a solid financial house. It MUST start with a STRONG & STURDY foundation to avoid the inevitable trials of everyday life.

Building a <u>Solid</u> Financial House

Estate Planning

Wealth & Retirement Accumulation

Debt Freedom

Rainy Day Fund

Budget Creation

Income Protection/Will Preparation

*Turn the page &
let's start building!*

The Foundation: Income Protection

A solid foundation is a way to ensure longevity and   strength. A solid foundation helps the rest of the structure remain upright. The first building block in your financial house is protecting what's YOURS. You've worked HARD for your money. So, it only makes sense, to provide adequate protection for your income and your family. Oftentimes, we get an emotional and spiritual high and run down to the altar to give our **10%** without first devising a solid plan. So, as you begin this financial journey…as you begin to plot out your plan…Ask yourself, "**When I leave this life, will I leave my family UNprotected?**" When you die, your loved ones will have to deal with the emotional stress of you being absent from their lives.

PLEASE! PLEASE! PLEASE! Don't burden them with the ghosts of your current poor financial decisions.

"So how do I make certain that my family is protected after I am gone?"

I am SOOO glad that you asked!

The Foundation: Income Protection

A good rule of thumb is to have at LEAST **10 TIMES** your annual income in a term life insurance policy. Why? If you're the main source of income for your family and you're dead and cannot work, they'll have to figure out how to make ends meet.

Mom may have to deliver pizza, get an overnight job, or sell a kidney!

So, with **10 TIMES** your annual income being delivered to your family upon your demise, your family can continue to maintain the same standard of living as they did while you were alive.

Let's look at an example: Meet Robert.

An Example: Robert's Story

Meet Robert. He works as a Financial Planner and makes $80,000 per year. Robert has a wife who also works, but he is still the breadwinner. Robert and his wife have a child who is beginning travel baseball. Robert seems like a decent man and would like to properly plan for his family before he is ready to meet his Creator. He goes and talks to an insurance agent.

Let's calculate how much life insurance Robert will need:

Robert's annual income is: $80,000.

Robert's income **x10** is: $800,000.

Robert wants a basic funeral, which would cost his family around $11,000.

Robert and his wife have a mortgage with a remaining balance of $75,000.

The total life insurance that Robert should have is $886,000.
($800,000 + 11,000 + 75,000)

In other words,

1. Robert's family can **maintain their same standard of living for 10 years**;

2. Robert's family can **bury him WORRY-FREE**;

3. Robert's family can **pay off his debt**.

Why? Because he **TOOK CARE OF BUSINESS!!**

"*A prudent person* plans ahead and will foresee dangers and avoid them, but the foolish person (a non-planner) will rush ahead, do whatever's convenient, and end up suffering the consequences."

- Proverbs 22:3

So, how much life insurance should YOU have?

Use the Life Insurance Calculator on the next page to figure it out!

Life Insurance Calculator

Do you have children/dependents? [Skip to the next page if you chose NO]

☐ Yes ☐ No

The money you take home after taxes.

1) My current *annual net income* is

   $_____.

2) My current annual net income times **10** is

   $_____.

3) Through my **research**, I have found that in order for me to be **buried (or cremated)** it will cost my family

   $_____.

4) The TOTAL **debt** that I currently owe is

   $_____.

Idealistically, the amount of life insurance that I should have is

$_____

[Add your answers from Questions 2 - 4].

I do NOT have children/dependents.

1) Through my **research**, I have found that in order for me to be **buried (or cremated)** it will cost my family

$_____.

2) The TOTAL **debt** that I currently owe is

$_____.

3) I would like to leave my family with

$_____.

Idealistically, the amount of life insurance that I should have is

$_____

[Add your answers from Questions 1 - 3].

Way to go! Now that you've laid a strong foundation, it's time to build on that success. Financial freedom is a process—trust it. Step by step. Brick by brick. Let's move forward with The First Brick: Budgeting.

But don't begin until you count the costs. For who would begin construction of a building without first calculating the costs to see if there is enough money to finish it? Otherwise, you might complete only the foundation before running out of money, and then everyone would laugh at you. They would say, "There's the person who started that building and couldn't afford to finish it."

- Luke 14:28-30

The First Brick: Budgeting

Creating a **budget** is a firm way to take control of your money. With a budget, you can tell your money exactly where to go, rather than looking back and wondering where it went.

Where Do I Start?

1. **Write down your total after-tax income.**

   This is the amount of money that you bring home from your job, self-employment income, (LEGAL) side hustles, etc.

Source	Amount
Employment Income	$
Side Hustle 1	$
Side Hustle 2	$
Dividend Income	$
Interest	$
Self-Employment Income	$

Budgeting does not have to be intimidating. Conversely, it's a NECESSARY activity for individuals and families.

The First Brick: Budgeting

And Then What?

2. List ALL of your monthly expenses.

Essentials	
Rent/Mortgage	$
Gas	$
Electricity	$
Water	$
Clothing (Self)	$
Clothing (Kids)	$
Groceries	$
Restaurants	$
Car Insurance	$
Life Insurance	$

Expenses should include your regular expenses (mortgage, utilities, car note, etc.) and your irregular expenses (home repairs, insurances, homeowners' association dues, lawn care, etc.) that are due in the upcoming period. ALL expenses should be accounted for, including food, entertainment, and gas. This should also include your savings & investments as well.

The First Brick: Budgeting

Financial Priorities

Savings	$
Tithes/Charitable Giving	$
Investments	$
Retirement	$
Kid's Savings	$
Credit Card Payment 1 (hopefully ZERO)	$
Credit Card Payment 2 (hopefully ZERO)	$
Car Note	$
Student Loan	$

The First Brick: Budgeting

3. Your Bottom Line Should be ZERO.

Zero-based budgeting means that your income minus your expenses should equal zero.

Lifestyle Choices

Phone	$
Travel	$
Cable TV	$
Memberships	$
Dues/Subscriptions	$
Shopping	$
Leisure Activity 1	$
Leisure Activity 2	$

> This does <u>NOT</u> mean you are broke or that you spent your entire paycheck. What it does mean is that you know WHERE all your money is going.
> It means you are in control and that you are telling your money exactly where it needs to go.

The First Brick: Budgeting

4. Track Your Expenses

This step will ensure you are sticking to your budget. Remember to hold yourself accountable and stick to the plan!

*This can also help you figure out what expenses can be **cut** from the budget.*

NOTE!!

We included LEISURE/FUN activities into our budget.

What does that tell us?
It is OKAY to enjoy your hard-earned money.
The budget allows you to proactively manage where you want your money to go & not wondering where it has gone!

Rainy Day/ "FEMA" Fund

49% of Americans could cover less than 1 month's expenses if they lost their income.

We've all been hit with unexpected expenses at some point in our lives. With proper planning, those expenses will sting a little less. Just like FEMA and the Red Cross are always prepared to respond to an emergency, so should you and your household. When a crisis hits America, they have a response team on the scene ASAP! While they may not make the emergency go away, they alleviate the burden, pain, and suffering until people are able to get back on their feet.

Proper planning promotes prosperity.

What unexpected expenses have affected your household lately?

- Flat Tire
- Sick Child
- Hospital Stay
- Car Breakdown
- ER Visit
- Job Loss
- Etc. Etc. Etc.

Rainy Day/ "FEMA" Fund
Emergency Preparedness Plan

1. Begin with putting **$1,000** to the side in an interest-bearing savings account that isn't too easy to access.

2. Aim for 6 months of expenses.

    a) My total monthly expenses are

       $_____.

    b) My monthly expenses **times 6** is

       $_____.

    By having 6 months of expenses placed into a savings account, you can ensure that in the event of an extended period of unemployment, you can continue paying your expenses for at least 6 months without any additional income.

That was easy! Now, on the next few pages, let's discuss everybody's not-so-favorite topic...
DEBT!

"The rich rule over the poor, and the <u>borrower is slave to the lender</u>."

- Proverbs 22:7

Debt Freedom
What is **debt**?

An amount of money **borrowed** by one party from another generally used to make large purchases that **could not be afforded under normal circumstances.**

Many people in debt typically got there by substituting **saving** for a large purchase with **acquiring debt** (swiping that credit card, signing up for low introductory rates, trying the "same as cash" payment plan).

Debt Freedom

Before getting yourself into a debt
situation, ask yourself:
Can I afford it?

If I cannot afford it, then
Do I really need it?

It's soul-searching time!

In order to BE debt free, it is important

to SEE yourself debt free!

*Take a moment and imagine life without
debt...*

What would you feel like if you had absolutely NO DEBT?

What would you do with your income if you had ZERO debt payments?

How old were you when you got your 1st credit card? How did it make you feel?

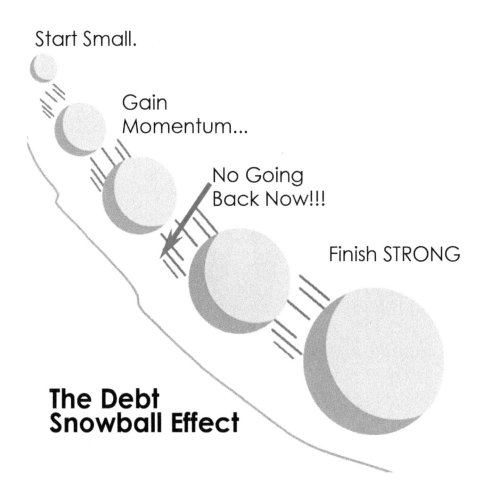

Start Small.

Gain
Momentum...

No Going
Back Now!!!

Finish STRONG

**The Debt
Snowball Effect**

Debt Freedom
The Snowball Effect

So, what can you do to combat debt? I'll answer that in 3 simple steps:

1. Start **SMALL**

2. Gain **MOMENTUM**

3. Finish **STRONG**

Start by paying the smallest obligation **first**. *Keep your goals simple and celebrate the small wins. Pick up steam and move to the next debt. Keep it going until your final debt obligation is **ZERO**!*

Read on to take a closer look at the Snowball Effect. —>

Debt Freedom
The Snowball Effect

Snowball example:

Debt Name	Beginning Balance	Current Payment	New Payment	# of Payments
Debt 1	$705.00	$25.00	$135.00	5.2
Debt 2	$882.00	$29.00	$164.00	5.4
Debt 3	$1,598.00	$59.00	$223.00	7.2
Debt 4	$2,751.89	$72.00	$295.00	9.3
Debt 5	$3,104.39	$86.00	$381.00	8.1

Now you give it a try!!
—>

Debt Freedom
The Snowball Effect

Debt Name *Give it a name. Make it personal.*	Balance *How much do I owe on it Today?*	Current Minimum Monthly Payment	New Payment *After budgeting, how much extra money can I apply to paying off debt?*	# of Payments to FREEDOM *Divide the beginning balance by the new payment*

Wealth Accumulation & Retirement Planning

Proverbs 13:11 – *"Wealth gained hastily will dwindle, but whomever gathers little by little will increase it."*

Deuteronomy 8:1 – *"The whole commandment that I command you today shall be careful to do, that you may live and multiply, and go in and possess the land that the Lord swore to give your fathers."*

At one point or another in our lives, we've all thought about retiring, sitting on a beach and watching sunsets. Sadly, most of us may not believe that this could be our REALITY. The good news is: With proper planning, you CAN retire wealthy and retire at a point in your life where you can still enjoy the fruits of your labor. WHEN you follow the financial literacy program and very strategically build up your wealth, you can retire comfortably!

Wealth Accumulation & Retirement Planning
Building Blocks to a Sturdy Retirement

☐ 401K/403B

- *Employee makes **pre-tax** payroll contributions.*

- *Sometimes an employer matches contribution up to a certain percentage.*

*If your employer matches your contributions, it may be a good idea to take advantage of that FREE money! Think about it this way ...If you contribute 3% and your employer matches 3%, that is an immediate **100% return**!*

☐ IRA (Individual Retirement Account)

- **Traditional IRA**
  - ❖ "Pre-Tax" Contributions
  - ❖ Withdrawals are taxed at your normal tax rate at the time of the withdrawal(s).
  - ❖ There is a minimum retirement age (as of 2019, that age is 59 ½)
    There are penalties for early withdrawals (prior to reaching the minimum age).

- **ROTH IRA**
  - ❖ Contributions made "after-tax"
  - ❖ Earnings and withdrawals are tax-free
  - ❖ Best if you anticipate being in a higher tax bracket in retirement

It IS a good idea to have both IRA types. There are solid strategies that can be employed during retirement for additional tax savings. However, if you decide to contribute to both, the annual contribution limit still applies & is NOT doubled.

Wealth Accumulation & Retirement Planning

Max out employer sponsored 401K/403B plan (up to the employer match)

Contribute excess funds to IRA depending on your current & future tax brackets, up to the annual limit.

If there is no employer match, then begin with funding the IRA.

Estate Planning

Proverbs 13:22 – *"A good man leaves an inheritance to his children's children…"*

1 Timothy 5:8 – *"But if anyone does not provide for his relatives, and especially for members of his household, he has denied the faith and is worse than an unbeliever."*

Making a lot of money and having everything you desire while you are living is nice and all. But what type of legacy are you leaving behind. Here's a little secret…**Everyone has an estate**. Your estate is everything that you own: your car, house, life insurance, investments, furniture, and personal possessions. Proper estate planning will take the path with the least amount paid in legal fees, taxes, and court costs.

If you fail to properly plan, your state may have a plan for you that you won't like!
Having a <u>will</u> in place is a good start to your estate planning.

Estate Planning

Last Will & Testament

A **Will**:

- Is a legal document of a person's wishes upon death;

- Identifies assets: property and possessions; and identifies recipients of those assets (beneficiaries).

Who should have a will? YOU!

A law office is a good place to start when looking to put a will into place.

When you plan ahead, there is money left to give generously.

Proverbs 28:27 – *"Whomever gives to the poor will not want, but he who hides his eyes will get many a curse."*

Ecclesiastes 10:19 – *"Bread is made for laughter, and wine gladdens life, and **MONEY** answers everything!"*

Proverbs 13:18 – *"Poverty and disgrace come to him who ignores instruction, but whomever heeds reproof is honored."*

I thoroughly believe that when you give, it is returned to you tenfold. Call it karma, blessings, etc. etc. Whatever you want to call it, just **GIVE** and do so freely. However, we HAVE to take the proper steps AND take them in the proper order.

Note: You CANNOT give money that you do not have! With that said, let's devise a plan, stick to the plan, and be disciplined in the approach.

The Financial Literacy Pledge

Your name here

I, _____ , hereby pledge my entire being to developing a better financial future for myself, my family, and generations to come. I, furthermore pledge to discontinue digging a debt grave and will learn to destroy debt and accumulate wealth.

Beginning TODAY, I will make informed financial decisions, while understanding the difference between wants and needs. I will be consciously aware of the effects of advertisements on my decision-making process and resolve not to be influenced by them. I will focus on my financial health by tracking my expenses and creating a budget that is REALISTIC. I will continue my education regarding personal debt, saving, investing, budgeting, and credit. I will be proactive in my planning for periodic expenses, including holidays. I will lead by example; teaching my children the importance of expense management, saving, budgeting, and the wise use of credit. I will no longer let fear and shame prevent me from talking about my financial well-being and seek the necessary help to fix it.

The Financial Literacy Pledge

From this day forth, I will not make excuses for my behavior and will no longer make poor financial decisions. I am, by signing below, stating my intention to not only abide by the terms of this contract, but to re-read this document whenever I am tempted to make a poor or brash financial decision.

This contract is valid only when signed by at least one witness and must be kept in a place where I can view it daily.

Signed: **Dated:**

_____   _____

Witness(es):

_____

Assets =
What you **OWN**

Liabilities=
What you **OWE**

Net Worth = Assets minus Liabilities

Try it!

ASSETS	
Cash	$
Savings Account(s)	$
Checking Account(s)	$
Certificates of Deposit (CD)	$
Other Savings Vehicles (i.e. savings bond)	$
Life Insurance, cash value	$
Annuities, Surrender Value	$
Brokerage Account	$
Mutual Fund	$
Stocks & Bonds	$
Rental Property	$
Keogh	$
Sep IRA	$
Traditional IRA	$
ROTH IRA	$
401K/403B	$
Profit Sharing	$
Pension Plan	$
Market Value of Primary Home	$
Market Value of Vehicle	$
Jewelry/Precious Metals/Gemstones	$
Collectibles	$
Furnishings/Art	$
Other Assets	$
TOTAL ASSETS	**$**

Nine Tenth

LIABILITIES	
Mortgage(s) – Balance	$
Car Loan(s) – Balance	$
Credit Card(s) – Balance	$
Student Loan(s) – Balance	$
Back-Taxes Owed	$
Line(s) of Credit	$
Investment Debt (Margin)	$
Other Debt (Things owed)	$
TOTAL LIABILITIES	$
NET WORTH (TOTAL ASSETS minus TOTAL LIABILITIES)	$

Nine Tenth

For more information on Financial Freedom and to keep up with Dr. Clement Ogunyemi

Visit

www.4QFinancial.com

Connect

clement.ogunyemi@4QFinancial.com

LinkedIn - Dr. Clement Ogunyemi

Follow

Facebook - www.facebook.com/4QFinancial

Instagram - @drclemento

4Q Pro Financial Management & Consulting, LLC

CPSIA information can be obtained
at www.ICGtesting.com
Printed in the USA
BVHW021931091219
565925BV00003B/2/P

9 780578 551067